# What's in this book

This book belongs to

_____

# 郑和下西洋 Zheng He's voyages

## 学习内容 Contents

### 沟通 Communication

说说旅行经历
**Talk about travel experiences**

说说服装
**Talk about clothes**

### 生词 New words

| | | |
|---|---|---|
| ★ | 从 | from |
| ★ | 到 | to |
| ★ | 旅行 | to travel |
| ★ | 国家 | country |
| ★ | 出发 | to set out |
| ★ | 短裤 | shorts |
| ★ | 大衣 | coat |
| ★ | 毛衣 | sweater, jumper |
| | 年轻 | young |
| | 事情 | affair |
| | 漂亮 | beautiful |
| | 衬衫 | shirt |

从 1405 年到 1433 年，他进行了七次航海旅行。
He had seven sea voyages from 1405 to 1433.

从中国到美国，我可以坐飞机。
I can travel by air from China to America.

**跨学科学习 Project**

调查上海天气并设计旅行计划
Research the weather in Shanghai
and plan a trip

**文化 Cultures**

中西方城市的标志性建筑
Landmarks of cities in the East
and the West

# Get ready

**1** Do you like travelling? Why?

**2** Have you travelled by ship before?

**3** Do you know the man in the picture?

shì qíng
事情

nián qīng
年轻

你认识这个年轻人吗？你知道中国
古代郑和航海的事情吗？

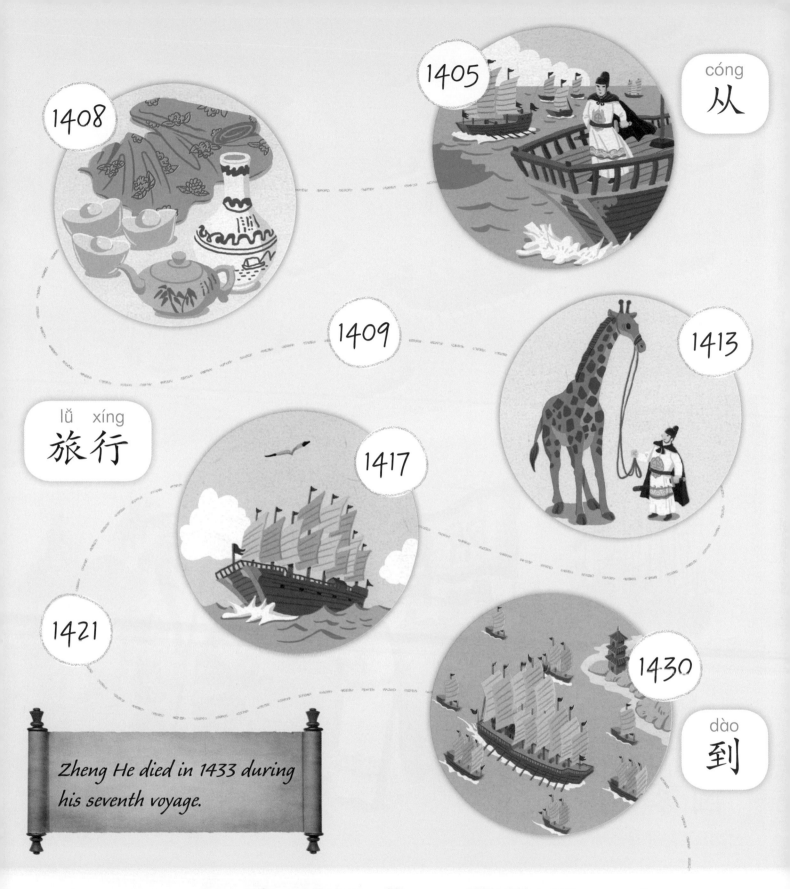

1408

1405

cóng
从

1409

1413

lǚ xíng
旅行

1417

1421

1430

dào
到

*Zheng He died in 1433 during his seventh voyage.*

从1405年到1433年，郑和用二十八年的时间，进行了七次航海旅行。

国家

他带领二百四十多只船，去了三十多个国家和地区。

出发

你想像郑和一样，从你的国家出发，探索大陆和大海吗？

pìao liang
漂亮

从这个国家到那个国家，我们可以
看漂亮的风景。

大衣 dà yī

毛衣 máo yī

衬衫 chèn shān

短裤 duǎn kù

去旅行，应该穿短裤还是大衣？衬衫还是毛衣？做好准备会更完美。

# Let's think

**1** Recall the story. Circle the correct answers.

1     Where did Zheng He start each voyage?

    a 中国        b 英国        c 美国

2     When did Zheng He start his first voyage?

    a 1433        b 1408        c 1405

3     How many countries and regions did Zheng He go to?

    a 十多个        b 二十多个        c 三十多个

**2** Discuss your favourite way to travel with your friend. You may draw your own idea.

你喜欢怎么去旅行？

我喜欢坐……去旅行。因为……

# New words

**02** **1** Learn the new words.

出发

Departures ✈

大衣

毛衣

漂亮

从 国家 到

年轻

短裤

旅行

衬衫

事情

**2** Listen to your teacher and point to the correct words above.

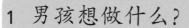 **1** Listen and circle the correct answers.

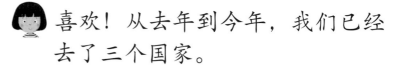 **2** Look at the pictures. Listen to the story an

**1** 男孩想做什么？

　a 跳舞

　b 唱歌

　c 旅行

**2** 男孩从哪个国家出发？

　a 英国

　b 美国

　c 中国

**3** 男孩不会带什么衣服？

　a 大衣

　b 毛衣

　c 短裤

 你们喜欢旅行吗？

喜欢！从去年到今年，我们已经去了三个国家。

 下雨了，我们去那边。

 雨真大！

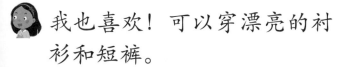 我最喜欢夏天去有海的国家。

我也喜欢！可以穿漂亮的衬衫和短裤。

妈妈，你怎么知道会下雨？

因为我做好了准备。

他们从哪里出发？

北京

他们从……出发。

从家里到操场，她们怎么去？

她们……

她穿了什么衣服？

她穿了……

# Task

Paste a photo of your favourite trip. Talk about it with your friend.

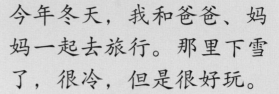
去年，我们从美国出发，去英国旅行。英国的城市很漂亮。

今年冬天，我和爸爸、妈妈一起去旅行。那里下雪了，很冷，但是很好玩。

Paste your photo here.

……年，我从……到……我最喜欢……

# Game

Play with your friend. Pick a card and say the word aloud. Ask your friend to say the opposite.

老 哭 年轻 高 长

冷 短 热 笑 矮

哭

# Chant

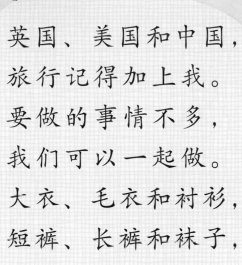

英国、美国和中国，
旅行记得加上我。
要做的事情不多，
我们可以一起做。
大衣、毛衣和衬衫，
短裤、长裤和袜子，
大家一起准备好。
出发旅行带背包，
开心一笑拍拍照。

## 生活用语 Daily expressions

够了吗？
Is that enough?

让我来。
Let me do it.

# 写一写 Write

## 1  Trace and write the characters.

丿 亻 亼 从

从　从　从　从

亠 屮 出 出

一 ナ 方 发 发

出　发　出　发

## 2  Write and say.

＿＿去年到今年，我去了很多地方。

我们一起＿＿去旅行了。

**3** Fill in the blanks with the correct words. Colour the clothes using the same colours.

从　　出发　　衣　　雨

今天＿＿＿＿＿＿前，妈妈说："你看看窗外的天气，可能会下＿＿＿。"我穿上毛＿＿和雨＿＿，准备了＿＿伞。＿＿家里＿＿＿＿＿＿后，已经开始下＿＿了。

## 拼音输入法 Pinyin input

Write the Pinyin above the words with the leaves and type the paragraph. Check with your friends to see who can finish first.

今年秋天，我们坐船去中国旅行。

我最喜欢秋天，因为风景很漂亮。我可以穿我喜欢的大衣和毛衣。我们学了功夫，看见了熊猫，还知道了很多中国的事情。

# 多元学习 Connections

## Cultures

Every big city has something interesting to see. Learn about the landmarks below. Which one would you like to visit? Tell your friend about it.

从美国到中国，我们可以坐飞机。我想去北京旅行，去看看……

### Beijing, China

The Forbidden City, located in the centre of Beijing, was home to the 24 emperors of the Ming and the Qing dynasties.

### Agra, India

The Taj Mahal, a marble building, was commissioned by a Mughal emperor in memory of his wife.

它真漂亮，你想去吗？

它非常高。很多人知道它。你喜欢这个国家吗？

### Paris, France

The Eiffel Tower, an iron tower named after its engineer Gustave Eiffel, is 324 metres tall. It is the icon of France.

### New York, United States

The Statue of Liberty, a sculpture of the female figure Libertas, is the icon of freedom and of the United States.

这个城市真大！

**1** Talk about a holiday you had and show a photo to your friend.

……年，我去……旅行了。那里很漂亮，天气非常好。我穿衬衫和……去。从我的城市到那里，坐……最舒服。去旅行是我最喜欢的事情。

Paste your photo here.

**2** Plan a trip to Shanghai during your favourite season. Research the weather and complete the table below. You may use some words more than once. Then tell your friend about your plan.

a 毛衣　b 短裤　c 大衣　d 衬衫　e 围巾

我想……去上海旅行，因为天气很……我……月从……出发。我会穿……和……我可以玩……

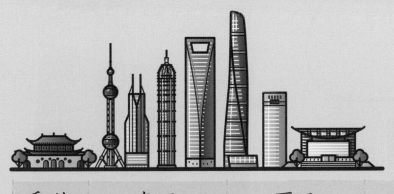

| 季节 | 春天 | 夏天 | 秋天 | 冬天 |
|------|------|------|------|------|
| 天气 | 5–18°C | _____°C | _____°C | _____°C |
| 衣服 | | | | |

# 温习 Checkpoint

**1** Help the boy complete his holiday journal. Read what he says and write the characters.

8月1日

今天不太热，我和朋友一起去学校打篮球。

8月3日

我最喜欢的事情是骑自行车。上午，我骑自行车去看电影。

8月7日

我的阿姨很年轻，也很快乐。

我买了大衣和毛衣，还买了漂亮的 …… 和 ……

8月12日

我们 ☐☐ 家里 ☐☐ ，一起去中国旅行。

8月17日

8月22日

中国是我最想去的国家。从北京到上海，我们去了很多地方。

**2** Work with your friend. Colour the stars and the chillies.

| Words | 说 | 读 | 写 |
|---|---|---|---|
| 从 | ☆ | ☆ | ☆ |
| 到 | ☆ | ☆ | 🌶 |
| 旅行 | ☆ | ☆ | 🌶 |
| 国家 | ☆ | ☆ | 🌶 |
| 出发 | ☆ | ☆ | ☆ |
| 短裤 | ☆ | ☆ | 🌶 |
| 大衣 | ☆ | ☆ | 🌶 |
| 毛衣 | ☆ | ☆ | 🌶 |
| 年轻 | ☆ | 🌶 | 🌶 |
| 事情 | ☆ | 🌶 | 🌶 |

| Words and sentences | 说 | 读 | 写 |
|---|---|---|---|
| 漂亮 | ☆ | 🌶 | 🌶 |
| 衬衫 | ☆ | 🌶 | 🌶 |
| 从 1405 年到 1433 年，他进行了七次航海旅行。 | ☆ | 🌶 | 🌶 |
| 从中国到美国，我可以坐飞机。 | ☆ | 🌶 | 🌶 |

| | |
|---|---|
| Talk about travel experiences | ☆ |
| Talk about clothes | ☆ |

**3** What does your teacher say?

My teacher says ...

21

# 分享 Sharing

## Words I remember

| | | |
|---|---|---|
| 从 | cóng | from |
| 到 | dào | to |
| 旅行 | lǚ xíng | to travel |
| 国家 | guó jiā | country |
| 出发 | chū fā | to set out |
| 短裤 | duǎn kù | shorts |
| 大衣 | dà yī | coat |
| 毛衣 | máo yī | sweater, jumper |
| 年轻 | nián qīng | young |
| 事情 | shì qing | affair |
| 漂亮 | piào liang | beautiful |
| 衬衫 | chèn shān | shirt |

# Other words

| | | |
|---|---|---|
| 郑和 | zhèng hé | Zheng He |
| 西洋 | xī yáng | Western Seas |
| 认识 | rèn shi | to know |
| 古代 | gǔ dài | ancient times |
| 航海 | háng hǎi | navigation |
| 进行 | jìn xíng | to proceed |
| 次 | cì | time |
| 带领 | dài lǐng | to lead |
| 地区 | dì qū | area |
| 探索 | tàn suǒ | to explore |
| 大陆 | dà lù | continent |
| 风景 | fēng jǐng | scenery |
| 应该 | yīng gāi | should |
| 准备 | zhǔn bèi | to prepare |
| 更 | gèng | even more |
| 完美 | wán měi | perfect |

# OXFORD
UNIVERSITY PRESS

Oxford University Press is a department of the University of Oxford.
It furthers the University's objective of excellence in research, scholarship,
and education by publishing worldwide. Oxford is a registered trade mark of
Oxford University Press in the UK and in certain other countries

Published in Hong Kong by
Oxford University Press (China) Limited
39th Floor, One Kowloon, 1 Wang Yuen Street, Kowloon Bay,
Hong Kong

Illustrated by Ah Lun, Anne Lee, Emily Chan, KY Chan and Wildman

Photographs for reproduction permitted by Dreamstime.com

China National Publications Import & Export (Group) Corporation is an authorized distributor of
Oxford Elementary Chinese.

Please contact content@cnpiec.com.cn or 86-10-65856782

ISBN: 978-0-19-047009-8

10 9 8 7 6 5 4 3 2